Fremdsprachentexte

Robert Louis Stevenson
The Bottle Imp

Herausgegeben von
Dieter Hamblock

Philipp Reclam jun. Stuttgart

Universal-Bibliothek Nr. 9157

Gesamtherstellung: Reclam, Ditzingen. Printed in Germany 2002

ISBN 3-15-009157-8

www.reclam.de

The Bottle Imp

There was a man of the Island of Hawaii, whom I shall call Keawe; for the truth is, he still lives, and his name must be kept secret; but the place of his birth was not far from Honaunau, where the bones of Keawe the Great lie hidden in a cave. This man was poor, brave, and active; he could read and write like a schoolmaster; he was a first-rate mariner besides, sailed for some time in the island steamers, and steered a whale boat on the Hamakua coast. At length it came in Keawe's mind to have a sight of the great world and foreign cities, and he shipped on a vessel bound to San Francisco.

This is a fine town, with a fine harbour, and rich people uncountable; and, in particular, there is one hill which is covered with palaces. Upon this hill Keawe was one day taking a walk with his pocket full of money, viewing the great houses upon either hand with pleasure. 'What fine houses these are!' he was thinking, 'and how happy must those people be who dwell in them, and take no care for the morrow!' The thought was in his mind when he came abreast of a house that was smaller than some others, but all finished and beautiful like a toy; the steps

1 **imp:** Kobold, Teufelchen.
9 **whale** (zool.): Wal.
12 **bound to:** hier: anstelle des heute geläufigen *bound for* ›mit dem Zielhafen‹.
20 **morrow:** ausschließlich literarische Variante von *morning*.
21 **abreast:** in gleicher Höhe.

of that house shone like silver, and the borders of the garden bloomed like garlands, and the windows were bright like diamonds; and Keawe stopped and wondered at the excellence of all he saw. So stopping, he was aware of a man that looked forth upon him through a window so clear that Keawe could see him as you see a fish in a pool upon a reef. The man was elderly, with a bald head and a black beard, and his face was heavy with sorrow, and he bitterly sighed. And the truth of it is, that as Keawe looked in upon the man, and the man looked out upon Keawe, each envied the other.

All of a sudden, the man smiled and nodded, and beckoned Keawe to enter, and met him at the door of the house.

'This is a fine house of mine,' said the man, and bitterly sighed. 'Would you not care to view the chambers?'

So he led Keawe all over it, from the cellar to the roof, and there was nothing there that was not perfect of its kind, and Keawe's was astonished.

'Truly,' said Keawe, 'this is a beautiful house; if I lived in the like of it, I should be laughing all day long. How comes it, then, that you should be sighing?'

'There is no reason,' said the man, 'why you should not have a house in all points similar to this, and finer, if you wish. You have some money, I suppose?'

'I have fifty dollars,' said Keawe, 'but a house like this will cost more than fifty dollars.'

1 **border:** Rand; hier: Ränder der Gartenbeete.
2 **garland:** Girlande, Blumengewinde.
7 **reef:** (Felsen-)Riff.
8 **bald:** kahl.
11 **to envy:** beneiden.
13 **to beckon:** (herbei)winken.

The man made a computation. 'I am sorry you have no more,' said he, 'for it may raise you trouble in the future, but it shall be yours at fifty dollars.'

'The house?' asked Keawe.

'No, not the house,' replied the man, 'but the bottle. For, I must tell you, although I appear to you so rich and fortunate, all my fortune, and this house itself and its garden, came out of a bottle not much bigger than a pint. This is it.'

And he opened a lockfast place, and took out a round-bellied bottle with a long neck; the glass of it was white like milk, with changing rainbow colours in the grain. Withinsides something obscurely moved, like a shadow and a fire.

'This is the bottle,' said the man; and, when Keawe laughed, 'You do not believe me?' he added. 'Try, then, for yourself. See if you can break it.'

So Keawe took the bottle up and dashed it on the floor till he was weary; but it jumped on the floor like a child's ball, and was not injured.

'This is a strange thing,' said Keawe. 'For by the touch of it, as well as by the look, the bottle should be glass.'

'Of glass it is,' replied the man, sighing more heavily than ever, 'but the glass of it was tempered in the flames

1 **computation:** Berechnung.
9 **pint:** Pinte (0,57 l).
10 **lockfast:** verschlossen.
11 **bellied:** von *belly* ›Bauch‹.
12 **grain:** wörtl.: Korn; hier: Gewebe, Fasern.
13 **obscurely** (adv.): dunkel; undeutlich.
18 **to dash:** schleudern; zerschlagen.
19 **weary:** müde, überdrüssig.
20 **to injure:** verletzen, beschädigen.
24 **to temper:** härten.

of hell. An imp lives in it, and that is the shadow we behold there moving; or so I suppose. If any man buy this bottle the imp is at his command; all that he desires – love, fame, money, houses like this house, ay, or a city like this city – all are his at the word uttered. Napoleon had this bottle, and by it he grew to be the king of the world; but he sold it at the last, and fell. Captain Cook had this bottle, and by it he found his way to so many islands; but he, too, sold it, and was slain upon Hawaii. For once it is sold, the power goes and the protection; and unless a man remain content with what he has, ill will befall him.'

'And yet you talk of selling it yourself?' Keawe said.

'I have all I wish, and I am growing elderly,' replied the man. 'There is one thing the imp cannot do – he cannot prolong life; and, it would not be fair to conceal from you, there is a drawback to the bottle; for if a man die before he sells it, he must burn in hell for ever.'

'To be sure, that is a drawback and no mistake,' cried Keawe. 'I would not meddle with the thing. I can do without a house, thank God; but there is one thing I

2 **to behold:** sehen.
if any man buy: noch im 19. Jh. geläufige Konjunktivform in Konditionalsätzen; vgl. 6,11 *unless a man remain;* 6,18 *if a man die.*
4 **ay:** ja.
5 **to utter:** äußern, aussprechen.
9 **to slay:** erschlagen.
17 **to prolong:** verlängern.
to conceal: verbergen.
18 **drawback:** Kehrseite, Nachteil.
21 **no mistake:** hier: daran besteht kein Zweifel.
22 **to meddle:** sich einmischen; sich abgeben.

could not be doing with one particle, and that is to be damned.'

'Dear me, you must not run away with things,' returned the man. 'All you have to do is to use the power of the imp in moderation, and then sell it to someone else, as I do to you, and finish your life in comfort.'

'Well, I observe two things,' said Keawe. 'All the time you keep sighing like a maid in love, that is one; and, for the other, you sell this bottle very cheap.'

'I have told you already why I sigh,' said the man. 'It is because I fear my health is breaking up; and, as you said yourself, to die and go to the devil is a pity for anyone. As for why I sell so cheap, I must explain to you there is a peculiarity about the bottle. Long ago, when the devil brought it first on earth, it was extremely expensive, and was sold first of all to Prester John for many millions of dollars; but it cannot be sold at all, unless sold at a loss. If you sell it for as much as you paid for it, back it comes to you again like a homing pigeon. It follows that the price has kept falling in these centuries, and the bottle is now remarkably cheap. I bought it myself from one of my great neighbours on this hill, and the price I paid was only ninety dollars. I could sell it for as high as eighty nine dollars and ninety cents, but not a penny dearer, or back the thing must come to me. Now, about this there are two bothers. First, when you offer a

1 **particle:** Teilchen; hier redensartlich: *not ... with one particle* ›keinen Funken, keineswegs, überhaupt nicht‹.
5 **moderation:** Mäßigung, Maß.
14 **peculiarity:** Eigentümlichkeit.
16 **Prester John:** mittelalterliche Legendenfigur eines angeblich im Orient herrschenden christlichen Königs oder Priesters.
26 **bother:** Ärgernis, Problem.

bottle so singular for eighty odd dollars people suppose you to be jesting. And second – but there is no hurry about that – and I need not go into it. Only remember it must be coined money that you sell it for.'

'How am I to know that this is all true?' asked Keawe.

'Some of it you can try at once,' replied the man. 'Give me your fifty dollars, take the bottle, and wish your fifty dollars back into your pocket. If that does not happen, I pledge you my honour I will cry off the bargain and restore your money.'

'You are not deceiving me?' said Keawe.

The man bound himself with a great oath.

'Well, I risk that much,' said Keawe, 'for that can do no harm.' And he paid over his money to the man, and the man handed him the bottle.

'Imp of the bottle,' said Keawe, 'I want my fifty dollars back.' And sure enough he had scarce said the word before his pocket was as heavy as ever.

'To be sure this is a wonderful bottle,' said Keawe.

'And now good morning to you, my fine fellow, and the devil go with you for me!' said the man.

'Hold on,' said Keawe, 'I don't want any more of this fun. Here, take your bottle back.'

'You have bought it for less than I paid for it,' replied the man, rubbing his hands. 'It is yours now; and, for my part, I am only concerned to see the back of you.' And with that he rang for his Chinese servant, and had Keawe shown out of the house.

Now, when Keawe was in the street with the bottle

1 **eighty odd dollars:** etwas über achtzig Dollar.
9 **to pledge:** verpfänden; verbürgen.
bargain: Geschäft.

under his arm, he began to think. 'If all is true about this bottle, I may have made a losing bargain,' thinks he. 'But perhaps the man was only fooling me.' The first thing he did was to count his money; the sum was exact – forty nine dollars American money, and one Chili piece. 'That looks like the truth,' said Keawe. 'Now I will try another part.'

The streets in that part of the city were as clean as a ship's decks, and though it was noon, there were no passengers. Keawe set the bottle in the gutter and walked away. Twice he looked back, and there was the milky, round-bellied bottle where he left it. A third time he looked back, and turned a corner; but he had scarce done so, when something knocked upon his elbow, and, behold! it was the long neck sticking up; and as for the round belly, it was jammed into the pocket of his pilot coat.

'And that looks like the truth,' said Keawe.

The next thing he did was to buy a corkscrew in a shop, and go apart into a secret place in the fields. And there he tried to draw the cork, but as often as he put the screw in, out it came again, and the cork as whole as ever.

'This is some new kind of cork,' said Keawe, and all at once he began to shake and sweat, for he was afraid of the bottle.

On this way back to the portside, he saw a shop where a man sold shells and clubs from the wild islands, old

5f. **Chili piece:** chilenisches Geldstück, etwas weniger als ein amerikanischer Dollar wert.

10 **gutter:** Gosse.

16 **to jam:** pressen, zwängen.

18 **corkscrew:** Korkenzieher.

27 **club:** Keule.

heathen deities, old coined money, pictures from China and Japan, and all manner of things that sailors bring in their seachests. And here he had an idea. So he went in and offered the bottle for a hundred dollars. The man of the shop laughed at him at the first, and offered him five; but, indeed, it was a curious bottle – such glass was never blown in any human glassworks, so prettily the colours shone under the milky white, and so strangely the shadow hovered in the midst; so, after he had disputed awhile after the manner of his kind, the shopman gave Keawe sixty dollars for the thing, and set it on a shelf in the midst of his window. 'Now,' said Keawe, 'I have sold that for sixty which I bought for fifty – or, to say the truth, a little less, because one of my dollars was from Chili. Now I shall know the truth upon another point.'

So he went back on board his ship, and, when he opened his chest, there was the bottle, and had come more quickly than himself. Now Keawe had a mate on board whose name was Lopaka.

'What ails you,' said Lopaka, 'that you stare in your chest?'

They were alone in the ship's forecastle, and Keawe bound him to secrecy, and told all.

'This is a very strange affair,' said Lopaka; 'and I fear you will be in trouble about this bottle. But there is one point very clear – that you are sure of the trouble, and you had better have the profit in the bargain. Make up

1 **heathen deity:** heidnische Gottheit, Götzenbild.
3 **seachest:** Seekiste.
9 **to hover:** schweben.
21 **to ail:** schmerzen.
23 **forecastle:** Vorderdeck.

your mind what you want with it; give the order, and if it is done as you desire, I will buy the bottle myself; for I have an idea of my own to get a schooner, and go trading through the islands.'

'That is not my idea,' said Keawe, 'but to have a beautiful house and garden on the Kona Coast, where I was born, the sun shining in at the door, flowers in the garden, glass in the windows, pictures on the walls, and toys and fine carpets on the tables, for all the world like the house I was in this day – only a storey higher, and with balconies all about like the King's palace; and to live there without care and make merry with my friends and relatives.'

'Well,' said Lopaka, 'let us carry it back with us to Hawaii; and if all comes true, as you suppose, I will buy the bottle, as I said, and ask a schooner.'

Upon that they were agreed, and it was not long before the ship returned to Honolulu, carrying Keawe and Lopaka and the bottle. They were scarce come ashore when they met a friend upon the beach who began at once to condole with Keawe.

'I do not know what I am to be condoled about,' said Keawe.

'Is it possible you have not heard,' said the friend, 'your uncle – that good old man – is dead, and your cousin that beautiful boy – was drowned at sea?'

Keawe was filled with sorrow, and, beginning to weep and to lament, he forgot about the bottle. Lopaka was

3 **schooner:** Schoner (Schiff).
10 **storey:** Stockwerk.
16 **to ask:** hier: in Auftrag geben, bauen lassen.
21 **to condole with s. o.:** jdn. bemitleiden.
26 **to be drowned** (auch: *to drown*): ertrinken.

thinking to himself, and presently when Keawe's grief was a little abated, 'I have been thinking,' said Lopaka. 'Had not your uncle lands in Hawaii, in the district of Kaü?'

'No,' said Keawe, 'not in Kaü; they are on the mountainside – a little way south of Hookena.'

'These lands will now be yours?' asked Lopaka.

'And so they will,' says Keawe, and began again to lament for his relatives.

'No,' said Lopaka, 'do not lament at present. I have a thought in my mind. How if this should be the doing of the bottle? For here is the place ready for your house.'

'If this be so,' cried Keawe, 'it is a very ill way to serve me by killing my relatives. But it may be, indeed, for it was in just such a station that I saw the house with my mind's eye.'

'The house, however, is not yet built,' said Lopaka.

'No, nor like to be!' said Keawe, 'for though my uncle has some coffee and ava and bananas, it will not be more than will keep me in comfort; and the rest of that land is the black lava.'

'Let us go to the lawyer,' said Lopaka, 'I have still this idea in my mind.'

Now, when they came to the lawyer's, it appeared Keawe's uncle had grown monstrous rich in the last days, and there was a fund of money.

2 **to be abated** (auch: *to abate*): nachlassen.
16 **station:** Standort.
19 **like:** anstelle der heute üblichen Form *likely*.
20 **ava** (bot.): pazifische Palmfrucht, aus der ein alkoholisches Getränk destilliert wird.
23 **lawyer:** Rechtsanwalt, Notar.

'And here is the money for the house!' cried Lopaka.

'If you are thinking of a new house,' said the lawyer, 'here is the card of a new architect, of whom they tell me great things.'

'Better and better!' cried Lopaka. 'Here is all made plain for us. Let us continue to obey orders.'

So they went to the architect, and he had drawings of houses on his table.

'You want something out of the way,' said the architect, 'How do you like this?' and he handed a drawing to Keawe.

Now, when Keawe set eyes on the drawing, he cried out aloud, for it was the picture of his thought exactly drawn.

'I am in for this house,' thought he. 'Little as I like the way it comes to me, I am in for it now, and I may as well take the good along with the evil.'

So he told the architect all that he wished, and how he would have that house furnished, and about the pictures on the wall and the knick-knacks on the table; and he asked the man plainly for how much he would undertake the whole affair.

The architect put many questions, and took his pen and made a computation; and when he had done he named the very sum that Keawe had inherited.

Lopaka and Keawe looked at one another and nodded.

10 **out of the way:** hier: ungewöhnlich, besonders.
16 **in:** hier: vorherbestimmt, festgelegt.
21 **knick-knacks:** Kleinigkeiten; Ornamente, Nippes.
26 **to inherit:** erben.

'It is quite clear,' thought Keawe, 'that I am to have this house, whether or no. It comes from the devil, and I fear I will get little good by that; and of one thing I am sure, I will make no more wishes as long as I have this bottle. But with the house I am saddled, and I may as well take the good along with the evil.'

So he made his terms with the architect, and they signed a paper; and Keawe and Lopaka took ship again and sailed to Australia; for it was concluded between them they should not interfere at all, but leave the architect and the bottle imp to build and to adorn that house at their own pleasure.

The voyage was a good voyage, only all the time Keawe was holding in his breath, for he had sworn he would utter no more wishes, and take no more favours from the devil. The time was up when they got back. The architect told them that the house was ready, and Keawe and Lopaka took a passage in the *Hall*, and went down Kona way to view the house, and see if all had been done fitly according to the thought that was in Keawe's mind.

Now, the house stood on the mountainside, visible to ships. Above, the forest ran up into the clouds of rain; below, the black lava fell in cliffs, where the kings of old lay buried. A garden bloomed about that house with every hue of flowers; and there was an orchard of

5 **to saddle:** satteln; hier: sich wohl versehen.
9 **to conclude:** beschließen.
10 **to interfere:** sich einmischen.
11 **to adorn:** schmücken, verzieren.
13 **voyage:** Seereise.
18 **Hall:** Name des Schiffes (›Halle‹).
25 **hue:** Farbton.
orchard: Obstgarten.

papaia on the one hand and an orchard of breadfruit on the other, and right in front, toward the sea, a ship's mast had been rigged up and bore a flag. As for the house, it was three storeys high, with great chambers and broad balconies on each. The windows were of glass, so excellent that it was as clear as water and as bright as day. All manner of furniture adorned the chambers. Pictures hung upon the wall in golden frames: pictures of ships, and men fighting, and of the most beautiful women, and of singular places; nowhere in the world are these pictures of so bright a colour as those Keawe found hanging in his house. As for the knick-knacks, they were extraordinary fine; chiming clocks and musical boxes, little men with nodding heads, books filled with pictures, weapons of price from all quarters of the world, and the most elegant puzzles to entertain the leisure of a solitary man. And as no one would care to live in such chambers, only to walk through and view them, the balconies were made so broad that a whole town might have lived upon them in delight; and Keawe knew not which to prefer, whether the back porch, where you got the land breeze, and looked upon the orchards and the flowers, or the front balcony, where you could drink the wind of the sea, and look down the steep wall of the mountain and see the *Hall* going by once a week or so between Hookena and

1 **papaia** (bot.): tropische Baumfrucht.
3 **to rig up:** aufstellen, aufrichten.
13 **to chime:** läuten.
14 **musical box:** Spieluhr.
17 **solitary:** einsam, alleinstehend.
22 **porch:** Säulenhalle (Portikus); hier: Veranda.
25 **steep:** steil.

the hills of Pele, or the schooners plying up the coast for wood and ava and bananas.

When they had viewed all, Keawe and Lopaka sat on the porch.

'Well,' asked Lopaka, 'is it all you designed?'

'Words cannot utter it,' said Keawe. 'It is better than I dreamed, and I am sick with satisfaction.'

'There is but one thing to consider,' said Lopaka; 'all this may be quite natural, and the bottle imp have nothing whatever to say to it. If I were to buy the bottle, and got no schooner after all, I should have put my hand in the fire for nothing. I gave you my word, I know; but yet I think you would not grudge me one more proof.'

'I have sworn I would take no more favours,' said Keawe. 'I have gone already deep enough.'

'This is no favour I am thinking of,' replied Lopaka. 'It is only to see the imp himself. There is nothing to be gained by that, and so nothing to be ashamed of; and yet, if I once saw him, I should be sure of the whole matter. So indulge me so far, and let me see the imp; and, after that, here is the money in my hand, and I will buy it.'

'There is only one thing I am afraid of,' said Keawe. 'The imp may be very ugly to view; and if you once set eyes upon him you might be very undesirous of the bottle.'

'I am a man of my word,' said Lopaka. 'And here is the money betwixt us.'

1 **to ply up:** regelmäßig (be)fahren.
5 **to design:** ersinnen, entwerfen.
13 **to grudge:** mißgönnen.
20 **to indulge:** gewähren (lassen).
28 **betwixt:** andere Form für *between*.

'Very well,' replied Keawe. 'I have a curiosity myself. So come, let us have one look at you, Mr. Imp.'

Now as soon as that was said, the imp looked out of the bottle, and in again, swift as a lizard; and there sat Keawe and Lopaka turned to stone. The night had quite come, before either found a thought to say or voice to say it with; and then Lopaka pushed the money over and took the bottle.

'I am a man of my word,' said he, 'and had need to be so, or I would not touch this bottle with my foot. Well, I shall get my schooner and a dollar or two for my pocket; and then I will be rid of this devil as fast as I can. For, to tell you the plain truth, the look of him has cast me down.'

'Lopaka,' said Keawe, 'do not you think any worse of me than you can help; I know it is night, and the roads bad, and the pass by the tombs an ill place to go by so late, but I declare since I have seen that little face, I cannot eat or sleep or pray till it is gone from me. I will give you a lantern, and a basket to put the bottle in, and any picture or fine thing in all my house that takes your fancy – and be gone at once, and go sleep at Hookena with Nahinu.'

'Keawe,' said Lopaka, 'many a man would take this ill; above all, when I am doing you a turn so friendly, as to keep my word and buy the bottle; and for that matter, the night and the dark, and the way by the tombs, must

4 **lizard:** Eidechse.

9f. **and had need to be so:** und mußte (es) notgedrungen sein; freier: und (ich) habe (mein Wort) immer gehalten.

12 **to be rid of s. th.:** etwas los sein.

13f. **to cast down:** niederwerfen, bedrücken.

17 **tomb:** Grab(mal).

be all tenfold more dangerous to a man with such a sin upon his conscience, and such a bottle under his arm. But for my part, I am so extremely terrified myself, I have not the heart to blame you. Here I go then; and I pray God you may be happy in your house, and I fortunate with my schooner, and both get to Heaven in the end in spite of the devil and his bottle.'

So Lopaka went down the mountain; and Keawe stood in his front balcony, and listened to the clink of the horse's shoes, and watched the lantern go shining down the path, and along the cliff of caves where the old dead are buried; and all the time he trembled and clasped his hands, and prayed for his friend, and gave glory to God that he himself was escaped out of that trouble.

But the next day came very brightly, and that new house of his was so delightful to behold that he forgot his terrors. One day followed another, and Keawe dwelt there in perpetual joy. He had his place on the back porch; it was there he ate and lived, and read the stories in the Honolulu newspapers; but when anyone came by they would go in and view the chambers and the pictures. And the fame of the house went far and wide; it was called *Ka-Hale Nui* – the Great House – in all Kona; and sometimes the Bright House, for Keawe kept a Chinaman, who was all day dusting and furbishing; and the glass, and the gilt, and the fine stuffs, and the pictures, shone as bright as the morning. As for

1 **tenfold:** zehnfach.
9 **clink:** Geklapper.
12 **to clasp:** klammern, falten.
18 **perpetual:** fortwährend.
25 f. **to furbish:** putzen, polieren.
26 **gilt:** Vergoldung, vergoldete Gegenstände.

Keawe himself, he could not walk in the chambers without singing, his heart was so enlarged; and when ships sailed by upon the sea, he would fly his colours on the mast.

So time went by, until one day Keawe went upon a visit as far as Kailua to certain of his friends. There he was well feasted; and left as soon as he could the next morning, and rode hard, for he was impatient to behold his beautiful house; and, besides, the night then coming on was the night in which the dead of old days go abroad in the sides of Kona; and having already meddled with the devil, he was the more chary of meeting with the dead. A little beyond Honaunau, looking far ahead, he was aware of a woman bathing in the edge of the sea; and she seemed a well grown girl, but he thought no more of it. Then he saw her white shift flutter as she put it on, and then her red holoku; and by the time he came abreast of her she was done with her toilet, and had come up from the sea, and stood by the trackside in her red holoku, and she was all freshened with the bath, and her eyes shone and were kind. Now Keawe no sooner beheld her than he drew his rein.

'I thought I knew every one in this country,' said he. 'How comes it that I do not know you?'

2 **to enlarge:** erweitern, vergrößern.
3 **to fly colours:** die Flagge hissen.
7 **to feast s.o.:** jdn. festlich bewirten.
8 **impatient:** ungeduldig.
12 **chary:** vorsichtig; ängstlich.
16 **shift:** (Frauen-)Unterhemd.
17 **holoku:** auf den Pazifikinseln übliches Gewand.
18 **toilet:** Ankleiden.
22 **rein:** Zügel.

'I am Kokua, daughter of Kiano,' said the girl, 'and I have just returned from Oahu. Who are you?'

'I will tell you who I am in a little,' said Keawe, dismounting from his horse, 'but not now. For I have a thought in my mind, and if you knew who I was, you might have heard of me, and would not give me a true answer. But tell me, first of all, one thing: Are you married?'

At this Kokua laughed out aloud. 'It is you who ask questions,' she said. 'Are you married yourself?'

'Indeed, Kokua, I am not,' replied Keawe, 'and never thought to be until this hour. But here is the plain truth. I have met you here at the roadside, and I saw your eyes which are like the stars, and my heart went to you as swift as a bird. And so now, if you want none of me, say so, and I will go to my own place; but if you think me no worse than any other young man, say so, too, and I will turn aside to your father's for the night, and tomorrow I will talk with the good man.'

Kokua said never a word, but she looked at the sea and laughed.

'Kokua,' said Keawe, 'if you say nothing, I will take that for the good answer; so let us be stepping to your father's door.'

She went on ahead of him, still without speech; only sometimes she glanced back and glanced away again, and she kept the strings of her hat in her mouth.

Now, when they had come to the door, Kiano came out on his veranda, and cried out and welcomed Keawe by name. At that the girl looked over, for the fame of the great house had come to her ears; and, to be sure, it was

15 **swift:** schnell.

a great temptation. All that evening they were very merry together; and the girl was as bold as brass under the eyes of her parents, and made a mock of Keawe, for she had a quick wit. The next day he had a word with Kiano, and found the girl alone.

'Kokua,' said he, 'you made a mock of me all the evening; and it is still time to bid me go. I would not tell you who I was, because I have so fine a house, and I feared you would think too much of that house and too little of the man who loves you. Now you know all, and if you wish to have seen the last of me, say so at once.'

'No,' said Kokua; but this time she did not laugh, nor did Keawe ask for more.

This was the wooing of Keawe; things had gone quickly; but so an arrow goes, and the ball of a rifle swifter still, and yet both may strike the target. Things had gone fast, but they had gone far also, and the thought of Keawe rang in the maiden's head; she heard his voice in the breach of the surf upon the lava, and for this young man that she had seen but twice she would have left father and mother and her native islands. As for Keawe himself, his horse flew up the path of the mountain under the cliff of tombs, and the sound of the hoofs, and the sound of Keawe singing to himself for pleasure,

1 **temptation:** Versuchung.
2 **bold:** kühn, keck.
brass: Messing.
3 **mock:** Hohn, Spott.
15 **to woo:** (Braut) werben.
16 **rifle:** Gewehr.
17 **target:** Ziel.
20 **surf:** Brandung.

echoed in the caverns of the dead. He came to the Bright House, and still he was singing. He sat and ate in the broad balcony, and the Chinaman wondered at his master, to hear how he sang between the mouthfuls. The sun went down into the sea, and the night came; and Keawe walked the balconies by lamplight, high on the mountains, and the voice of his singing startled men on ships.

'Here am I now upon my high place,' he said to himself. 'Life may be no better; this is the mountain top; and all shelves about me toward the worse. For the first time I will light up the chambers, and bathe in my fine bath with the hot water and the cold, and sleep alone in the bed of my bridal chamber.'

So the Chinaman had word, and he must rise from sleep and light the furnaces; and as he wrought below, beside the boilers, he heard his master singing and rejoicing above him in the lighted chambers. When the water began to be hot the Chinaman cried to his master; and Keawe went into the bathroom; and the Chinaman heard him sing as he filled the marble basin; and heard him sing, and the singing broken, as he undressed; until of a sudden, the song ceased. The Chinaman listened, and listened; he called up the house to Keawe to ask if

7 **to startle:** erschrecken.
11 **to shelve:** mit Fächern versehen; hier: herabfallen, nach unten gerichtet sein.
15 **So the Chinaman had word:** So wurde dem Chinesen befohlen.
16 **furnace:** Ofen.
wrought: altes Präteritum von *to work*.
17 **to rejoice:** sich freuen, jubeln.
21 **marble:** Marmor.
23 **to cease:** aufhören.

all were well, and Keawe answered him. 'Yes,' and bade him go to bed; but there was no more singing in the Bright House; and all night long, the Chinaman heard his master's feet go round and round the balconies without repose.

Now the truth of it was this: as Keawe undressed for his bath, he spied upon his flesh a patch like a patch of lichen on a rock, and it was then that he stopped singing. For he knew the likeness of that patch, and knew that he was fallen in the Chinese Evil – leprosy.

Now, it is a sad thing for any man to fall into this sickness. And it would be a sad thing for any one to leave a house so beautiful and so commodious, and depart from all his friends to the north coast of Molokai between the mighty cliff and seabreakers. But what was that to the case of the man Keawe, he who had met his love but yesterday, and won her but that morning, and now saw all his hopes break, in a moment, like a piece of glass?

Awhile he sat upon the edge of the bath; then sprang with a cry, and ran outside; and to and fro, to and fro, along the balcony, like one despairing.

'Very willingly could I leave Hawaii, the home of my fathers,' Keawe was thinking. 'Very lightly could I

5 **repose:** Ruhe.
7 **to spy:** erspähen.
patch: Flecken.
8 **lichen:** Flechte.
10f. **leprosy:** Aussatz.
14 **commodious:** geräumig.
15 **to depart:** Abschied nehmen.
22 **to and fro:** hin und her.

leave my house, the high-placed, the many-windowed, here upon the mountains. Very bravely could I go to Molokai, to Kalaupapa by the cliffs, to live with the smitten and to sleep there, far from my fathers. But what wrong have I done, what sin lies upon my soul, that I should have encountered Kokua coming cool from the seawater in the evening? Kokua, the soul ensnarer! Kokua, the light of my life! Her may I never wed, her may I look upon no longer, her may I no more handle with my loving hand; and it is for this, it is for you. O Kokua! that I pour my lamentations!'

Now you are to observe what sort of a man Keawe was, for he might have dwelt there in the Bright House for years, and no one been the wiser of his sickness; but he reckoned nothing of that, if he must lose Kokua. And again, he might have wed Kokua even as he was; and so many would have done, because they have the souls of pigs; but Keawe loved the maid manfully, and he would do her no hurt and bring her in no danger.

A little beyond the midst of the night, there came in his mind the recollection of that bottle. He went round to the back porch, and called to memory the day when the devil had looked forth; and at the thought ice ran in his veins.

4 **smitten:** von *to smite* ›schlagen, (schwer) treffen‹.
6 **to encounter:** begegnen.
8 **ensnarer:** Verführer(in).
9 **to wed:** heiraten.
10 **to handle:** handhaben; hier: berühren.
14 **to be the wiser of s. th.:** Kenntnis von etwas haben.
15 **to reckon:** rechnen, berücksichtigen.
18 **manfully** (adv.): männlich, mannhaft.
21 **recollection:** Erinnerung.
24 **vein:** Ader.

'A dreadful thing is the bottle,' thought Keawe, 'and dreadful is the imp, and it is a dreadful thing to risk the flames of hell. But what other hope have I to cure my sickness or to wed Kokua? What!' he thought, 'would I beard the devil once, only to get me a house, and not face him again to win Kokua?'

Thereupon he called to mind it was the next day the *Hall* went by on her return to Honolulu. 'There must I go first,' he thought, 'and see Lopaka. For the best hope that I have now is to find that same bottle I was so pleased to be rid of.'

Never a wink could he sleep; the food stuck in his throat; but he sent a letter to Kiano, and about the time when the steamer would be coming, rode down beside the cliff of the tombs. It rained; his horse went heavily; he looked up at the black mouths of the caves, and he envied the dead that slept there and were done with trouble; and called to mind how he had galloped by the day before, and was astonished. So he came down to Hookena, and there was all the country gathered for the steamer as usual. In the shed before the store they sat and jested and passed the news; but there was no matter of speech in Keawe's bosom, and he sat in their midst and looked without on the rain falling on the houses, and the surf beating among the rocks, and the sighs arose in his throat.

'Keawe of the Bright House is out of spirits,' said one to another. Indeed, and so he was, and little wonder.

1 **dreadful:** schrecklich.
5 **to beard:** mutig entgegentreten.
12 **wink:** Zwinkern, Augenblick.
17 **to be done with s. th.:** fertig sein mit etwas.
22 **to jest:** scherzen.

Then the *Hall* came, and the whaleboat carried him on board. The afterpart of the ship was full of Haoles (Whites) who had been to visit the volcano, as their custom is; and the midst was crowded with Kanakas, and the forepart with wild bulls from Hilo and horses from Kaü; but Keawe sat apart from all in his sorrow, and watched for the house of Kiano. There it sat, low upon the shore in the black rocks, and shaded by the cocoa palms, and there by the door was a red holoku, no greater than a fly, and going to and fro with a fly's business. 'Ah, queen of my heart,' he cried, 'I'll venture my dear soul to win you!'

Soon after, darkness fell, and the cabins were lit up, and the Haoles sat and played at the cards and drank whisky as their custom is; but Keawe walked the deck all night; and all the next day, as they steamed under the lee of Maui or of Molokai, he was still pacing to and fro like a wild animal in a menagerie.

Towards evening they passed Diamond Head, and came to the pier of Honolulu. Keawe stepped out among the crowd and began to ask for Lopaka. It seemed he had become the owner of a schooner – none better in the islands – and was gone upon an adventure as far as Pola-Pola or Kahiki; so there was no help to be looked for from Lopaka. Keawe called to mind a friend of his, a lawyer in the town (I must not tell his name), and inquired of him. They said he had grown suddenly rich, and had a fine new house upon Waikiki shore; and this

11 **to venture:** aufs Spiel setzen.
16 **lee:** Lee(seite), Windschatten.
17 **to pace:** schreiten.

put a thought in Keawe's head, and he called a hack and drove to the lawyer's house.

The house was all brand new, and the trees in the garden no greater than walking sticks, and the lawyer, when he came, had the air of a man well pleased.

'What can I do to serve you?' said the lawyer.

'You are a friend of Lopaka's,' replied Keawe, 'and Lopaka purchased from me a certain piece of goods that I thought you might enable me to trace.'

The lawyer's face became very dark. 'I do not profess to misunderstand you, Mr. Keawe,' he said, 'though this is an ugly business to be stirring in. You may be sure I know nothing, but yet I have a guess, and if you would apply in a certain quarter I think you might have news.'

And he named the name of a man, which, again, I had better not repeat. So it was for days, and Keawe went from one to another, finding everywhere new clothes and carriages, and fine new houses and men everywhere in great contentment, although to be sure, when he hinted at his business their faces would cloud over.

'No doubt I am upon the track,' thought Keawe. 'These new clothes and carriages are all the gifts of the little imp, and these glad faces are the faces of men who have taken their profit and got rid of the accursed thing in

1 **hack:** Mietpferd, Droschke.
5 **air:** Miene; Aussehen.
10 **to profess:** behaupten, heucheln.
12 **to stir:** (um)rühren.
13 **to apply:** sich hinwenden, sich umsehen.
19 **contentment:** Zufriedenheit.
20 **to hint:** andeuten, anspielen.
21 **track:** Spur.
24 **accursed:** verwünscht.

safety. When I see pale cheeks and hear sighing, I shall know that I am near the bottle.'

So it befell at last that he was recommended to a Haole in Beritania Street. When he came to the door, about the hour of the evening meal, there were the usual marks of the new house, and the young garden, and the electric light shining in the windows; when the owner came, a shock of hope and fear ran through Keawe; for here was a young man, white as a corpse, and black about the eyes, the hair shedding from his head, and such a look in his countenance as a man may have when he is waiting for the gallows.

'Here it is, to be sure,' thought Keawe, and so with this man he noways veiled his errand. 'I am come to buy the bottle,' said he.

At the word, the young Haole of Beritania Street reeled against the wall.

'The bottle!' he gasped. 'To buy the bottle!' Then he seemed to choke, and seizing Keawe by the arm carried him into a room and poured out wine in two glasses.

'Here is my respects,' said Keawe, who had been much about with Haoles in his time. 'Yes,' he added, 'I am come to buy the bottle. What is the price by now?'

9 **corpse:** Leiche.
11 **countenance:** Miene, Gesichtsausdruck.
12 **gallows** (pl.): Galgen.
14 **noways:** in keiner Weise.
to veil: verschleiern.
errand: Anliegen.
16 **to reel:** taumeln.
18 **to gasp:** keuchen.
19 **to choke:** ersticken, nach Luft schnappen.

At that word the young man let his glass slip through his fingers, and looked upon Keawe like a ghost.

'The price', says he; 'the price! You do not know the price?'

'It is for that I am asking you,' returned Keawe. 'But why are you so much concerned? Is there anything wrong about the price?'

'It has dropped a great deal in value since your time, Mr. Keawe,' said the young man, stammering.

'Well, well, I shall have the less to pay for it,' says Keawe. 'How much did it cost you?'

The young man was as white as a sheet. 'Two cents,' said he.

'What?' cried Keawe, 'two cents? Why, then, you can only sell it for one. And he who buys it —' The words died upon Keawe's tongue; he who bought it could never sell it again, the bottle and the bottle imp must abide with him until he died, and when he died must carry him to the red end of hell.

The young man of Beritania Street fell upon his knees. 'For God's sake buy it!' he cried. 'You can have all my fortune in the bargain. I was mad when I bought it at that price. I had embezzled money at my store; I was lost else; I must have gone to jail.'

'Poor creature,' said Keawe, 'you would risk your soul upon so desperate an adventure, and to avoid the proper punishment of your own disgrace; and you think I could hesitate with love in front of me. Give me the

9 **to stammer:** stammeln, stottern.
18 **to abide:** bleiben.
23 **to embezzle:** unterschlagen.
24 **jail:** Gefängnis.
27 **disgrace:** Schande.

bottle, and the change which I make sure you have all ready. Here is a five cent piece.'

It was as Keawe supposed; the young man had the change ready in a drawer; the bottle changed hands, and Keawe's fingers were no sooner clasped upon the stalk than he had breathed his wish to be a clean man. And, sure enough, when he got home to his room, and stripped himself before a glass, his flesh was whole like an infant's. And here was the strange thing: he had no sooner seen this miracle than his mind was changed within him, and he cared naught for the Chinese Evil, and little enough for Kokua; and had but the one thought, that here he was bound to the bottle imp for time and for eternity, and had no better hope but to be a cinder for ever in the flames of hell. Away ahead of him he saw them blaze with his mind's eye, and his soul shrank, and darkness fell upon the light.

When Keawe came to himself a little, he was aware it was the night when the band played at the hotel. Thither he went, because he feared to be alone; and there, among happy faces, walked to and fro, and heard the tunes go up and down, and saw Berger beat the

4 **drawer:** Schublade.
to change hands: den Besitzer wechseln.
6 **stalk:** Stengel, Flaschenhals.
8 **to strip:** abstreifen, (sich) ausziehen.
10 **miracle:** Wunder.
11 **naught:** nichts.
Chinese Evil: Lepra.
14 **eternity:** Ewigkeit.
15 **cinder:** Schlacke, Glut.
16 **to blaze:** lodern.
20 **thither:** dorthin.
22 **tune:** Melodie.

measure, and all the while he heard the flames crackle, and saw the red fire burning in the bottomless pit. Of a sudden the band played *Hiki-ao-ao*, that was a song that he had sung with Kokua, and at the strain courage returned to him.

'It is done now,' he thought, 'and once more let me take the good along with the evil.'

So it befell that he returned to Hawaii by the first steamer, and as soon as it could be managed he was wedded to Kokua, and carried her up the mountainside to the Bright House.

Now it was so with these two, that when they were together, Keawe's heart was stilled; but so soon as he was alone, he fell into a brooding horror, and heard the flames crackle, and saw the red fire burn in the bottomless pit. The girl, indeed, had come to him wholly; her heart leapt in her side at sight of him, her hand clung to his; and she was so fashioned from the hair upon her head to the nails upon her toes that none could see her without joy. She was pleasant in her nature. She had the good word always. Full of song she was, and went to and fro in the Bright House, the brightest thing in its three storeys, carolling like the birds. And Keawe beheld and heard her with delight, and then must shrink upon one side, and weep and groan to think upon the

1 **measure:** Maß; hier: Takt.
to crackle: knistern.
2 **pit:** Grube, Abgrund.
4 **strain:** hier: Melodie.
14 **to brood:** brüten.
17 **to cling:** sich anklammern, sich anschmiegen.
23 **to carol:** singen.
25 **to groan:** stöhnen.

price that he had paid for her; and then he must dry his eyes, and wash his face, and go and sit with her on the broad balconies, joining in her songs, and, with a sick spirit, answering her smiles.

There came a day when her feet began to be heavy and her songs more rare; and now it was not Keawe only that would weep apart, but each would sunder from the other and sit in opposite balconies with the whole width of the Bright House betwixt. Keawe was so sunk in his despair, he scarce observed the change and was only glad he had more hours to sit alone and brood upon his destiny, and was not so frequently condemned to pull a smiling face on a sick heart. But one day, coming softly through the house, he heard the sound of a child sobbing, and there was Kokua rolling her face upon the balcony floor, and weeping like the lost.

'You do well to weep in this house, Kokua,' he said. 'And yet I would give the head off my body that you (at least) might have been happy.'

'Happy!' she cried 'Keawe, when you lived alone in your Bright House, you were the word of the island for a happy man; laughter and song were in your mouth, and your face was as bright as the sunrise. Then you wedded poor Kokua; and the good God knows what is amiss in her – but from that day you have not smiled. 'Oh!' she cried, 'what ails me? I thought I was pretty,

7 **to sunder:** sich absondern.
12 **destiny:** Schicksal.
13 **to condemn:** verdammen.
25 f. **to be amiss:** fehlen, nicht stimmen.
27 **to ail:** schmerzen; hier: was fehlt (an) mir?; vgl. auch 32,25 f. *to be amiss*.

and I knew I loved him. What ails me that I throw this cloud upon my husband?'

'Poor Kokua,' said Keawe. He sat down by her side, and sought to take her hand; but that she plucked away. 'Poor Kokua,' he said, again. 'My poor child – my pretty. And I had thought all this while to spare you! Well, you shall know all. Then, at least, you will pity poor Keawe; then you will understand how much he loved you in the past – that he dared hell for your possession – and how much he loves you still (the poor condemned one), then he can yet call up a smile when he beholds you.'

With that, he told her all, even from the beginning.

'You have done this for me?' she cried. 'Ah, well, then what do I care!' – and she clasped and wept upon him.

'Ah, child!' said Keawe, 'and yet, when I consider of the fire of hell, I care a good deal!'

'Never tell me,' said she; 'no man can be lost because he loved Kokua, and no other fault. I tell you, Keawe, I shall save you with these hands, or perish in your company. What! you loved me, and gave your soul, and you think I will not die to save you in return?'

'Ah, my dear! you might die a hundred times, and what difference would that make?' he cried, 'except to leave me lonely till the time comes of my damnation?'

'You know nothing,' said she. 'I was educated in a school in Honolulu; I am no common girl. And I tell you, I shall save my lover. What is this you say about a

4 **to pluck:** zerren.
21 **to perish:** umkommen.
26 **damnation:** Verdammung.

cent? But all the world is not American. In England they have a piece they call a farthing, which is about half a cent. Ah! sorrow!' she cried, 'that makes it scarcely better, for the buyer must be lost, and we shall find none so brave as my Keawe! But, then, there is France; they have a small coin there which they call a centime, and these go five to the cent or thereabout. We could not do better. Come, Keawe, let us go to the French Islands; let us go to Tahiti, as fast as ships can bear us. There we have four centimes, three centimes, two centimes, one centime; four possible sales to come and go on; and two of us to push the bargain. Come, my Keawe! kiss me, and banish care. Kokua will defend you.'

'Gift of God!' he cried. 'I cannot think that God will punish me for desiring aught so good! Be it as you will, then; take me where you please: I put my life and my salvation in your hands.'

Early the next day Kokua was about her preparations. She took Keawe's chest that he went with sailoring; and first she put the bottle in a corner; and then packed it with the richest of their clothes and the bravest of the knick-knacks in the house. 'For,' said she, 'we must seem to be rich folks, or who will believe in the bottle?' All the time of her preparations she was as gay as a bird; only when she looked upon Keawe, the tears would spring in her eyes, and she must run and kiss him. As for Keawe, a weight was off his soul; now that he had his secret shared, and some hope in front of him, he

13 **to banish:** verbannen.
16 **aught:** (irgend) etwas.
18 **salvation:** Rettung.

seemed like a new man, his feet went lightly on the earth, and his breath was good to him again. Yet was terror still at his elbow; and ever and again, as the wind blows out a taper, hope died in him, and he saw the flames toss and the red fire burn in hell.

It was given out in the country they were gone pleasuring to the States, which was thought a strange thing, and yet not so strange as the truth, if they could have guessed it. So they went to Honolulu in the *Hall*, and thence in the *Umatilla* to San Francisco with a crowd of Haoles, and at San Francisco took their passage by the mail brigantine, the *Tropic Bird*, for Papeete, the chief place of the French in the south islands. Thither they came, after a pleasant voyage, on a fair day of the Trade Winds, and saw the reef with the surf breaking, and Motuiti with its palms, and the schooner riding withinside, and the white houses of the town low down along the shore among green trees, and overhead the mountains and the clouds of Tahiti, the wise island.

It was judged the most wise to hire a house, which they did accordingly, opposite the British Consul's, to make a great parade of money, and themselves conspicuous with carriages and horses. This it was very easy to

4 **taper:** Kerze.
5 **to toss:** (sich) hin und her werfen; hier: flackern.
7 **States:** The United States of America.
10 **thence:** von da.
12 **brigantine:** kleines Segelschiff.
15 **Trade Wind:** Passat.
22 f. **to make a parade:** eine Schau veranstalten; etwa: den Reichtum zur Schau stellen.
23 **conspicuous:** auffällig.

do, so long as they had the bottle in their possession; for Kokua was more bold than Keawe, and, whenever she had a mind, called on the imp for twenty or a hundred dollars. At this rate they soon grew to be remarked in the town; and the strangers from Hawaii, their riding and their driving, the fine holokus and the rich lace of Kokua, became the matter of much talk.

They got on well after the first with the Tahitian language, which is indeed like to the Hawaiian, with a change of certain letters; and as soon as they had any freedom of speech, began to push the bottle. You are to consider it was not an easy subject to introduce; it was not easy to persuade people you were in earnest, when you offered to sell them for four centimes the spring of health and riches inexhaustible. It was necessary besides to explain the dangers of the bottle; and either people disbelieved the whole thing and laughed, or they thought the more of the darker part, became overcast with gravity, and drew away from Keawe and Kokua, as from persons who had dealings with the devil. So far from gaining ground, these two began to find they were avoided in the town; the children ran away from them screaming, a thing intolerable to Kokua; Catholics crossed themselves as they went by, and all persons

7 **lace:** Schnur, Spitze; hier: Kokuas Spitzengewänder.
12 **to push:** stoßen; hier: abstoßen, zum Verkauf anbieten.
14 **to persuade:** überreden.
16 **inexhaustible:** unerschöpflich.
20 **gravity:** Ernsthaftigkeit, Bedenken.
24 **to scream:** schreien.
intolerable: unerträglich.

began with one accord to disengage themselves from their advances.

Depression fell upon their spirits. They would sit at night in their new house, after a day's weariness, and not exchange one word, or the silence would be broken by Kokua bursting suddenly into sobs. Sometimes they would pray together; sometimes they would have the bottle out upon the floor, and sit all the evening watching how the shadow hovered in the midst. At such times they would be afraid to go to rest. It was long ere slumber came to them, and if either dozed off, it would be to wake and find the other silently weeping in the dark, or, perhaps, to wake alone, the other having fled from the house and the neighbourhood of the bottle, to pace under the bananas in the little garden, or to wander on the beach by moonlight.

One night it was so when Kokua awoke. Keawe was gone. She felt in the bed and his place was cold. Then fear fell upon her, and she sat up in bed. A little moonshine filtered through the shutters. The room was bright, and she could spy the bottle on the floor. Outside it blew high, the great trees of the avenue cried aloud, and the fallen leaves rattled in the veranda. In the midst of this Kokua was aware of another sound; whether of a beast or of a man she could scarce tell,

1 **accord:** Einklang.
to disengage: lösen.
2 **advance:** Vormarsch, Fortschritt; hier etwa: Annäherungsversuch.
3 **depression:** Niedergeschlagenheit.
6 **sobs** (pl.): Schluchzen.
11 **slumber:** Schlummer.
to doze off: einschlafen.
20 **shutter:** Fensterläden.

but it was as sad as death, and cut her to the soul. Softly she arose, set the door ajar, and looked forth into the moonlit yard. There, under the bananas, lay Keawe, his mouth in the dust, and as he lay he moaned.

It was Kokua's first thought to run forward and console him; her second potently withheld her. Keawe had borne himself before his wife like a brave man; it became her little in the hour of weakness to intrude upon his shame. With the thought she drew back into the house.

'Heaven!' she thought, 'how careless have I been – how weak! It is he, not I, that stands in this eternal peril; it was he, not I, that took the curse upon his soul. It is for my sake, and for the love of a creature of so little worth and such poor help, that he now beholds so close to him the flames of hell – ay, and smells the smoke of it, lying without there in the wind and moonlight. Am I so dull of spirit that never till now I have surmised my duty, or have I seen it before and turned aside? But now, at least, I take up my soul in both the hands of my affection; now I say farewell to the white steps of heaven and the waiting faces of my friends. A love for a

2 **ajar:** halb geöffnet.
6 **to console:** trösten.
7 **potently** (adv.): stark.
to withhold: zurückhalten.
9 **to become:** werden; hier: geziemen.
9f. **to intrude upon s.o.:** jdn. stören.
13 **peril:** Gefahr.
18 **without:** hier: draußen.
19 **to surmise:** vermuten, erraten.
22 **affection:** Zuneigung.

love, and let mine be equalled with Keawe's! A soul for a soul, and be it mine to perish!'

She was a deft woman with her hands, and was soon apparelled. She took in her hands the change – the precious centimes they kept ever at their side; for this coin is little used, and they had made provision at a Government office. When she was forth in the avenue, clouds came on the wind and the moon was blackened. The town slept, and she knew not whither to turn till she heard one coughing in the shadow of the tree.

'Old man,' said Kokua, 'what do you here abroad in the cold night?'

The old man could scarce express himself for coughing, but she made out that he was old and poor, and a stranger in the island.

'Will you do me a service?' said Kokua. 'As one stranger to another, and as an old man to a young woman, will you help a daughter of Hawaii?'

'Ah,' said the old man. 'So you are the witch from the Eight Islands, and even my old soul you seek to entangle. But I have heard of you, and defy your wickedness.'

'Sit down here,' said Kokua, 'and let me tell you a tale.'

1 **to equal:** gleichmachen, gleichkommen.
3 **deft:** flink.
4 **apparelled:** angezogen.
6 **provision:** Vorkehrung.
9 **whither:** wohin.
11 **abroad:** draußen.
19 **witch:** Hexe.
21 **to entangle:** verstricken.
to defy: trotzen.
22 **wickedness:** Bösartigkeit.

And she told him the story of Keawe from the beginning to the end.

'And now,' said she, 'I am his wife, whom he bought with his soul's welfare. And what should I do? If I went to him myself and offered to buy it, he would refuse. But if you go, he will sell it eagerly; I will await you here: you will buy it for four centimes, and I will buy it again for three. And the Lord strengthen a poor girl!'

'If you meant falsely,' said the old man, 'I think God would strike you dead.'

'He would!' cried Kokua. 'Be sure he would. I could not be so treacherous – God would not suffer it.'

'Give me the four centimes and await me here,' said the old man.

Now, when Kokua stood alone in the street, her spirit died. The wind roared in the trees, and it seemed to her the rushing of the flames of hell; the shadows tossed in the light of the street lamp, and they seemed to her the snatching hands of evil ones. If she had had the strength, she must have run away, and if she had had the breath she must have screamed aloud; but, in truth, she could do neither, and stood and trembled in the avenue, like an affrighted child.

Then she saw the old man returning, and he had the bottle in his hand.

'I have done your bidding,' said he. 'I left your husband weeping like a child; tonight he will sleep easy.' And he held the bottle forth.

4 **welfare:** Wohlfahrt, Wohlergehen.
12 **treacherous:** betrügerisch.
19 **to snatch:** schnappen.
26 **bidding:** Geheiß.

'Before you give it to me,' Kokua panted, 'take the good with the evil – ask to be delivered from your cough.'

'I am an old man,' replied the other, 'and too near the gate of the grave to take a favour from the devil. But what is this? Why do you not take the bottle? Do you hesitate?'

'Not hesitate!' cried Kokua. 'I am only weak. Give me a moment. It is my hand resists, my flesh shrinks back from the accursed thing. One moment only!'

The old man looked upon Kokua kindly. 'Poor child!' said he, 'you fear; your soul misgives you. Well, let me keep it. I am old, and can never more be happy in this world, and as for the next —'

'Give it me!' gasped Kokua. 'There is your money. Do you think I am so base as that? Give me the bottle.'

'God bless you, child,' said the old man.

Kokua concealed the bottle under her holoku, said farewell to the old man, and walked off along the avenue, she cared not whither. For all roads were now the same to her, and led equally to hell. Sometimes she walked, and sometimes ran; sometimes she screamed out loud in the night, and sometimes lay by the wayside in the dust and wept. All that she had heard of hell came back to her; she saw the flames blaze, and she smelt the smoke, and her flesh withered on the coals.

Near day she came to her mind again, and returned to the house. It was even as the old man said – Keawe

1 **to pant:** keuchen.
12 **to misgive:** Böses ahnen lassen.
15 **to gasp:** keuchen.
16 **base:** gemein, niederträchtig.
26 **to wither:** verwelken, austrocknen.

slumbered like a child. Kokua stood and gazed upon his face.

'Now, my husband,' said she, 'it is your turn to sleep. When you wake it will be your turn to sing and laugh. But for poor Kokua, alas! that meant no evil – for poor Kokua no more sleep, no more singing, no more delight, whether in earth or Heaven.'

With that she lay down in the bed by his side, and her misery was so extreme that she fell in a deep slumber instantly.

Late in the morning her husband woke her and gave her the good news. It seemed he was silly with delight, for he paid no heed to her distress, ill though she dissembled it. The words stuck in her mouth, it mattered not; Keawe did the speaking. She ate not a bite, but who was to observe it? for Keawe cleared the dish. Kokua saw and heard him, like some strange thing in a dream; there were times when she forgot or doubted, and put her hands to her brow; to know herself doomed and hear her husband babble, seemed so monstrous.

All this while Keawe was eating and talking, and planning the time of their return, and thanking her for saving him, and fondling her, and calling her the true helper after all. He laughed at the old man that was fool enough to buy that bottle.

'A worthy old man he seemed,' Keawe said. 'But no

1 **to gaze:** starren.
13 **heed:** Aufmerksamkeit.
distress: Leid.
13 f. **to dissemble:** verbergen.
19 **to doom:** verdammen.
20 **to babble:** plappern, schwätzen.
23 **to fondle:** liebkosen.

one can judge by appearances. For why did the old reprobate require the bottle?'

'My husband,' said Kokua humbly, 'his purpose may have been good.'

Keawe laughed like an angry man.

'Fiddle-de-dee!' cried Keawe. 'An old rogue, I tell you; and an old ass to boot. For the bottle was hard enough to sell at four centimes; and at three it will be quite impossible. The margin is not broad enough, the things begins to smell of scorching – brrr!' said he, and shuddered. 'It is true I bought it myself at a cent, when I knew not there were smaller coins. I was a fool for my pains; there will never be found another; and whoever has that bottle now will carry it to the pit.'

'O my husband!' said Kokua. 'Is it not a terrible thing to save oneself by the eternal ruin of another? It seems to me I could not laugh. I would be humbled. I would be filled with melancholy. I would pray for the poor holder.'

Then Keawe, because he felt the truth of what she said, grew the more angry. 'Heighty-teighty!' cried he. 'You may be filled with melancholy if you please. It is not the mind of a good wife. If you thought at all of me, you would sit shamed.'

2 **reprobate:** Taugenichts.
6 **Fiddle-de-dee!:** etwa: Dummes Zeug!
rogue: Schurke.
7 **ass:** Esel.
to boot: obendrein.
9 **margin:** Spanne.
10 **to scorch:** versengen, verbrennen.
10f. **to shudder:** schaudern.
17 **to humble:** demütigen.
21 **Heighty-teighty!:** etwa: Was zum Teufel!

Thereupon he went out, and Kokua was alone.

What chance had she to sell that bottle at two centimes? None, she perceived. And if she had any, here was her husband hurrying her away to a country where there was nothing lower than a cent. And here – on the morrow of her sacrifice – was her husband leaving her and blaming her.

She would not even try to profit by what time she had, but sat in the house, and now had the bottle out and viewed it with unutterable fear, and now, with loathing, hid it out of sight.

By and by, Keawe came back, and would have her take a drive.

'My husband, I am ill,' she said. 'I am out of heart. Excuse me, I can take no pleasure.'

Then was Keawe more wroth than ever. With her, because he thought she was brooding over the case of the old man; with himself, because he thought she was right, and was ashamed to be so happy.

'This is your truth,' cried he, 'and this your affection! Your husband is just saved from eternal ruin, which he encountered for the love of you – and you can take no pleasure! Kokua, you have a disloyal heart.'

He went forth again furious, and wandered in the town all day. He met friends, and drank with them; they hired a carriage and drove into the country, and there drank again.

3 **to perceive:** wahrnehmen, feststellen.
10 **unutterable:** unsäglich.
loathing: Abscheu.
16 **wroth:** verärgert.
23 **disloyal:** treulos.
24 **furious:** wütend.

All the time Keawe was ill at ease, because he was taking his pastime while his wife was sad, and because he knew in his heart that she was more right than he; and the knowledge made him drink the deeper.

Now there was an old brutal Haole drinking with him, one that had been a boatswain of a whaler, a runaway, a digger in gold mines, a convict in prisons. He had a low mind and a foul mouth; he loved to drink and to see others drunken; and he pressed the glass upon Keawe. Soon there was no more money in the company.

'Here you!' says the boatswain, 'you are rich, you have been always saying. You have a bottle or some foolishness.'

'Yes,' says Keawe, 'I am rich; I will go back and get some money from my wife, who keeps it.'

'That's a bad idea, mate,' says the boatswain. 'Never you trust a petticoat with dollars. They're all as false as water; you keep an eye on her.'

Now, this word stuck in Keawe's mind; for he was muddled with what he had been drinking.

'I should not wonder but she was false, indeed,' thought he. 'Why else should she be cast down at my release? But I will show her I am not the man to be fooled. I will catch her in the act.'

Accordingly, when they were back in town, Keawe bade the boatswain wait for him at the corner, by the

1 **ill at ease:** unruhig.
2 **pastime:** Zeitvertreib.
6 **boatswain:** Bootsmann.
7 **convict:** Sträfling.
21 **to muddle:** verwirren.
23 **release:** Freilassung, Erlösung.

old calaboose, and went forward up the avenue alone to the door of his house. The night had come again; there was a light within, but never a sound, and Keawe crept around the corner, opened the back door softly, and looked in.

There was Kokua on the floor, the lamp at her side; before was a milk-white bottle, with a round belly and a long neck; and as she viewed it, Kokua wrung her hands.

A long time Keawe stood and looked in the doorway. At first he was struck stupid; and then fear fell upon him that the bargain had been made amiss, and the bottle had come back to him as it came at San Francisco; and at that his knees were loosened, and the fumes of the wine departed from his head like mists off a river in the morning. And then he had another thought; and it was a strange one, that made his cheeks to burn.

'I must make sure of this,' thought he.

So he closed the door, and went softly round the corner again, and then came noisily in, as though he were but now returned. And lo! by the time he opened the front door no bottle was to be seen; and Kokua sat in a chair and started up like one awakened out of sleep.

'I have been drinking all day and making merry,' said Keawe. 'I have been with good companions, and now I only come back for money, and return to drink and carouse with them again.'

1 **calaboose:** Gefängnis.
8 **to wring:** ringen.
14 **to loosen:** (sich) lösen.
fume: Dunst; hier: Rausch.
15 **mist:** Nebel.
27 **to carouse:** trinken, zechen.

Both his face and voice were as stern as judgment, but Kokua was too troubled to observe.

'You do well to use your own, my husband,' said she, and her words trembled.

'Oh, I do well in all things,' said Keawe, and he went straight to the chest and took out money. But he looked besides in the corner where they kept the bottle, and there was no bottle there.

At that the chest heaved upon the floor like a sea-billow, and the house span about like a wreath of smoke, for he saw he was lost now, and there was no escape. 'It is what I feared,' he thought; 'it is she who has bought it.'

And then he came to himself a little and rose up; but the sweat streamed on his face as thick as the rain and as cold as the well water.

'Kokua,' said he, 'I said to you today what ill became me. Now I return to carouse with my jolly companions,' and at that he laughed a little quietly. 'I will take more pleasure in the cup if you forgive me.'

She clasped his knees in a moment; she kissed his knees with flowing tears.

'Oh,' she cried, 'I asked but a kind word!'

'Let us never one think hardly of the other,' said Keawe, and was gone out of the house.

Now, the money that Keawe had taken was only some of that store of centime pieces they had laid at their

1 **stern:** ernst, finster.
judgment: i. S. v. *Last Judgment* ›Jüngstes Gericht‹.
10 **billow:** Woge.
to spin about: sich drehen, herumwirbeln.
wreath: Kranz.
24 **hardly:** hier: schlecht.

arrival. It was very sure he had no mind to be drinking. His wife had given her soul for him, now he must give his for her; no other thought was in the world with him.

At the corner, by the old calaboose, there was the boatswain waiting.

'My wife has the bottle,' said Keawe, 'and, unless you help me to recover it, there can be no more money and no more liquor tonight.'

'You do not mean to say you are serious about that bottle?' cried the boatswain.

'There is the lamp,' said Keawe. 'Do I look as if I was jesting?'

'That is so,' said the boatswain. 'You look as serious as a ghost.'

'Well, then,' said Keawe, 'here are two centimes; you must go to my wife in the house, and offer these for the bottle, which (if I am not much mistaken) she will give you instantly. Bring it to me here, and I will buy it back from you for one; for that is the law with this bottle, that it still must be sold for a less sum. But whatever you do, never breathe a word to her that you have come from me.'

'Mate, I wonder are you making a fool of me?' asked the boatswain.

'It will do you no harm if I am,' returned Keawe.

'That is so, mate,' said the boatswain.

'And if you doubt me,' added Keawe, 'you can try. As soon as you are clear of the house, wish to have your pocket full of money, or a bottle of the best rum, or what you please, and you will see the virtue of the thing.'

'Very well, Kanaka,' says the boatswain. 'I will try; but

if you are having your fun out of me, I will take my fun out of you with a belaying pin.'

So the whaler man went off up the avenue; and Keawe stood and waited. It was near the spot where Kokua had waited the night before; but Keawe was more resolved, and never faltered in his purpose; only his soul was bitter with despair.

It seemed a long time he had to wait before he heard a voice singing in the darkness of the avenue. He knew the voice to be the boatswain's; but it was strange how drunken it appeared upon a sudden.

Next, the man himself came stumbling into the light of the lamp. He had the devil's bottle buttoned in his coat; another bottle in his hand; and even as he came in view he raised it to his mouth and drank.

'You have it,' said Keawe. 'I see that.'

'Hands off!' cried the boatswain, jumping back. 'Take a step near me, and I'll smash your mouth. You thought you could make a catspaw of me, did you?'

'What do you mean?' cried Keawe.

'Mean?' cried the boatswain. 'This is a pretty good bottle, this is; that's what I mean. How I got it for two centimes I can't make out; but I'm sure you shan't have it for one.'

'You mean you won't sell?' gasped Keawe.

'No, *sir*!' cried the boatswain. 'But I'll give you a drink of the rum, if you like.'

2 **belaying pin:** Belegnagel.
6 **to falter:** schwanken, zögern.
18 **to smash:** zerschmettern, einschlagen.
19 **catspaw:** Handlanger.

'I tell you,' said Keawe, 'the man who has that bottle goes to hell.'

'I reckon I'm going anyway,' returned the sailor; 'and this bottle's the best thing to go with I've struck yet. No, sir!' he cried again, 'this is my bottle now, and you can go and fish for another.'

'Can this be true?' Keawe cried. 'For your own sake, I beseech you, sell it me!'

'I don't value any of your talk,' replied the boatswain. 'You thought I was a flat; now you see I'm not; and there's an end. If you won't have a swallow of the rum, I'll have one myself. Here's your health, and good night to you!'

So off he went down the avenue towards the town, and there goes the bottle out of the story.

But Keawe ran to Kokua light as the wind; and great was their joy that night; and great, since then, has been the peace of all their days in the Bright House.

3 **to reckon:** damit rechnen.
8 **to beseech:** ersuchen, anflehen.
10 **flat:** Trottel.
11 **swallow:** Schluck.

Editorische Notiz

Der englische Text folgt der Ausgabe *The Selected Writings of Robert Louis Stevenson*, New York: Random House, 1947. Das Glossar erklärt in der Regel alle Wörter, die über die Wertigkeitsstufe 2 des *Englischen Arbeitswörterbuches* von Alfred Haase (Frankfurt a. M.: Moritz Diesterweg, [7]1979) hinausgehen. Im Zweifelsfall wurde großzügig verfahren, d. h. eher eine Vokabel mehr aufgenommen als dort vorgesehen.

Literaturhinweise

Textausgaben

Gesamtausgaben

Edinburgh Edition, 28 Bde.; London 1894–98.
Vailima Edition, 26 Bde.; London 1922/23.
Tusitala Edition, 35 Bde.; London 1923/24.
South Seas Edition, 32 Bde.; New York 1925.

Anthologien, in denen auch *The Bottle Imp* erschienen ist

Island Nights Entertainments, London 1893.
Island Nights Entertainments, Pacific Classics Hawai 1975.
The Supernatural Stories, hrsg. von M. Hayes. London 1976.

Sekundärliteratur

F. Swinnerton, *R. L. Stevenson*, London 1915 (repr. 1966).
C. K. Chesterton, *Robert Louis Stevenson*, London 1927.
D. Daiches, *Robert Louis Stevenson*, Glasgow 1947.
C. B. Stern, *Robert Louis Stevenson*, London 1952.
E. M. Eigner, *Robert Louis Stevenson and Romantic Tradition*, Princeton 1966.
D. Daiches, *Robert Louis Stevenson and his world*, London 1973.
J. Pope Hennessy, *Robert Louis Stevenson*, London 1974.
I. S. Saposnitz, *Robert Louis Stevenson*, New York 1974.

Nachwort

Robert Louis Stevenson, weltweit bekannt als Autor von *Treasure Island* und *Dr. Jekyll and Mr. Hyde*, ist ein typischer Vertreter jener Generation viktorianischer Schriftsteller, die trotz ihres kurzen Lebens ein umfangreiches literarisches Gesamtwerk hinterließen. Die *Tusitala*-Ausgabe seiner Schriften – so genannt nach dem Ehrentitel »Tusitala« (etwa: der Erzähler), den ihm die Eingeborenen von Samoa als Anerkennung für seinen zunächst in der Landessprache verbreiteten *Bottle Imp* (1891) zuerkannten – umfaßt 35 Bände, und auch andere, weniger vollständige ›Gesamtausgaben‹ bestehen aus 20 und mehr Bänden. Kein Wunder, so will es scheinen, daß Stevenson vielfach als stellvertretend für die viktorianische Literatur, ja für den Viktorianismus schlechthin angesehen wurde. In George Orwells frühem Roman *Keep the Aspidistra Flying* (1936) läßt der in einem Buchladen arbeitende Romanheld Gordon Comstock seine antiviktorianischen und antischottischen Affekte bezeichnenderweise an Robert Louis Stevenson aus.

> »He glanced over their faded titles. *Collected Letters of Robert Louis Stevenson*. Ha, ha! That's good. *Collected Letters of Robert Louis Stevenson!* Its top edge was black with dust. Dust thou art, to dust thou returnest. Gordon kicked Stevenson's buckram backside. Art there, old false-penny? You're cold meat, if ever Scotchman was« (S. 15).

Die bei Orwell sicher exzessive, aber auch sonst eher ablehnende Reaktion auf das überwältigend erscheinende viktorianische Erbe führte später, etwa in der Mitte unseres Jahrhunderts, zu einer Vernachlässigung der viktorianischen Literatur in Kritik und Wissenschaft. Erst in neuerer Zeit hat man wieder begonnen, aus einer Distanz von etwa 100 Jahren die viktorianische Literatur einer Neubewertung zu unterziehen. Es ist gleichwohl bezeichnend für die ungebrochene Wirkung ihrer bedeutendsten Werke und Autoren, daß sie sich in all den Jahren und Jahrzehnten einer ungebrochenen Popularität erfreuten.

David Daiches hat sicher recht, wenn er die traditionelle, an der Biographie Stevensons orientierte Kritik als unzureichend für eine Würdigung seines literarischen Schaffens anprangert. Trotzdem weist Stevensons Lebensweg eine Reihe von Stationen auf, die bei der Erklärung seiner Schriften berücksichtigt werden müssen. Im übrigen erscheinen die unkonventionelle Biographie unseres Autors, seine zahlreichen Reisen und seine ihn auch physisch erschöpfende Rastlosigkeit geradezu als emblematisch für die Schriftsteller, ja vielleicht sogar die Gesellschaft jener Zeit.
Stevenson wurde 1850 in eine Familie hineingeboren, die den Idealvorstellungen der Epoche entsprach. Die in Edinburgh ansässigen Stevensons waren berühmte Leuchtturmbauer und standen religiös, nicht zuletzt durch verwandtschaftliche Verbindungen, in jener besonderen schottischen Ausprägung des Kalvinismus, die unterschwellig in Stevensons Werk vorhanden ist.
Die Karriere des jungen Robert Louis Stevenson – er verwendete später durchweg das Kürzel »R. L. S.« – als Ingenieur und Unternehmer schien vorherbestimmt. Doch zeigte sich bereits bei einem ersten Praktikum in der eigenen Firma, daß seine Gesundheit nicht robust genug war. Es folgte ein Jurastudium an der Universität Edinburgh. Obwohl er 1875 das angestrebte Berufsziel eines schottischen *barrister* erreichte, hatte sich Stevenson längst der Schriftstellerei verschrieben. Während seines Studiums erfuhr er durch Kontakte mit anderen Literaten sowie durch seine Europareisen Anregungen für Essays und Reisebeschreibungen, die nun in immer dichterer Folge verfaßt und publiziert wurden. 1876 verliebte er sich in Mrs. Osbourne, eine in Frankreich weilende Amerikanerin, der er wenige Jahre später nach Amerika folgte. Stevensons Eindrücke seiner Reise nach Kalifornien sind in *The Amateur Emigrant* (1895) und *Across the Plains* (1892) festgehalten, zwei auch heute noch häufig zitierte Reiseberichte. Die beschwerlichen Umstände dieser Unternehmung führten unseren Autor letztendlich zwar zu seiner Geliebten, hinterließen jedoch tiefe Spuren in seiner gesundheitlichen Verfassung.

In den folgenden Jahren pendelte das nunmehr verheiratete Paar zwischen Schottland, Davos, Paris und Südfrankreich. *Treasure Island* wurde in Schottland begonnen und 1882 in Davos abgeschlossen. Als Fortsetzungsgeschichte war diesem später berühmtesten Werk Stevensons kein besonderer Erfolg beschieden. Der Verkauf der Publikationsrechte für £ 100 an den Verleger Cassell erschien dem Autor mithin als großer Erfolg.
Ein wirklicher Durchbruch gelang erst mit *Dr. Jekyll and Mr. Hyde* (1886), einem Werk, das seinem Autor die gewünschte finanzielle Unabhängigkeit bescherte. In Amerika erschien diese Geschichte zwar in mehreren Raubdrucken, sorgte jedoch für die Bekanntheit ihres Verfassers. Dieser entschloß sich nach dem Tode seines Vaters zu einer Reise in die Vereinigten Staaten, wo er unter anderem auch eine Heilung seiner gesundheitlichen Gebrechen erhoffte. Schließlich führte eine von seinem amerikanischen Verleger finanzierte Südseereise zur letzten Station seines bewegten Lebens. Nach einem kurzen Aufenthalt in der Nähe von Honolulu landeten die Stevensons schließlich auf der Insel Opolu in der damals deutschen Kolonie Samoa. In der Ortschaft Apia erwarben sie Land und bauten sich ein Haus. Stevensons Einsatz für die Interessen der Eingeborenen brachte ihn in Konflikt mit den deutschen Kolonialbehörden, die gerade einen Aufstand niedergeschlagen hatten.
Die hier abgedruckte Erzählung *The Bottle Imp* sowie eine Reihe weiterer Südseegeschichten und -beschreibungen nehmen thematische oder zumindest topographische Elemente vorweg, die uns später bei Joseph Conrad, Joseph Rudyard Kipling und William Somerset Maugham wieder begegnen. Als Stevenson 1894 im Alter von 44 Jahren starb, hatte seine Popularität als Schriftsteller in seiner Heimat und der übrigen angelsächsischen Welt außergewöhnliche Höhen erreicht. Bis zum Ersten Weltkrieg erschienen nicht weniger als drei umfangreiche Gesamtausgaben seiner Werke sowie zahlreiche Editionen bislang weniger bekannter oder unveröffentlichter Schriften.

Unsere Erzählung *The Bottle Imp*, in deutschen Übersetzungen als *Flaschenkobold* (H. W. Draber, 1941) und *Flaschenteufelchen* (L. Wegener, 1955) bezeichnet, weist Bezüge zu den Gattungen Märchen und Fabel auf. Die englische Urfassung erschien 1893 in der Anthologie *Island Nights Entertainment*, deren Titel offenkundig eine Verbindung zu den bereits veröffentlichten Kurzgeschichtensammlungen *New Arabian Nights* (1882) und *More New Arabian Nights* (1885) herstellen sollte. Die ursprünglich orientalische Fabel vom Flaschenteufel wurde mit dieser Erzählung zunächst von einem Europäer für die Bewohner von Samoa umgeschrieben, erreichte dann jedoch in ihrer zwei Jahre später veröffentlichten englischen Urfassung wieder ein europäisches Publikum. Das schon in der ursprünglichen orientalischen Version enthaltene Motiv der Versuchung durch den Teufel – hier variiert durch eine erneute Versuchung und ein reichlich glückhaftes Ende für die der Versuchung Erlegenen – ist ein den Weltreligionen Judentum, Christentum und Islam gemeinsamer Mythos, der nicht nur in religiös erbaulichen Legenden, sondern auch in zahllosen säkularen Texten gestaltet wurde. Der Mythos und das von ihm geprägte Erzählmotiv gründen auf einer dualistischen Weltsicht, in der der mit Entscheidungsfreiheit ausgestattete Mensch allzu leicht dem nur irdische Güter bietenden Bösen verfallen kann und dabei die Gefahr ewiger Verdammnis aus seinem Bewußtsein verdrängt. Es wäre zweifellos überzogen, wollte man den zur Unterhaltung eingeborener Leser und Zuhörer geschriebenen *Bottle Imp* primär als Ausfluß eines stark dualistisch geprägten kalvinistischen Erbes deuten, dem sich Stevenson nicht zu entziehen vermochte. Ein Blick in sein übriges Erzählwerk zeigt jedoch, daß dieses Erbe mit seinen allegorischen Traditionen ihn häufig genug einen Konflikt zwischen Gut und Böse als Zentralmotiv von Erzählungen gestalten ließ. Ein weiteres kalvinistisches Motiv, das im *Bottle Imp* anklingt, ist das der Erwähltheit. In einer naiv säkularisierten Destillation dieses ehedem zentralen Glaubenssatzes wird hier dem Leser der Eindruck eines Protagonisten vermittelt, der letztendlich gewinnt, während ein anderer für die

Hölle prädestiniert ist. Keawe und seine Braut, die sich unserer Sympathie gewiß sein können, werden im Verlauf ihres Weges zum Glück, welches auch handfeste materielle Komponenten enthält, schwer geprüft, stehen am Ende gleichwohl als die Auserwählten da.
Der Handlungsablauf des *Bottle Imp* ist linear und, wie bei Kurzgeschichten allgemein üblich, ohne Nebenhandlungen. Die rasche Folge der einzelnen Episoden, der damit verbundene häufige Szenenwechsel und die im letzten Teil der Erzählung zwischen Keawe und Kokua alternierende Erzählperspektive sorgen – in Verbindung mit dem in Erwartung gestellten Höhepunkt – für die nötige Spannung, um einen Leser bei Laune zu halten, der auch sprachlich bescheidene Ansprüche hat. Hier paart sich die bei Stevenson übliche syntaktische Ökonomie mit einer ungewöhnlichen lexikalischen Beschränkung. Die sozusagen für eine Primärübersetzung in die Landessprache von Samoa erstellte englische Urfassung erwies sich im nachhinein als optimale Kinder- und Jugendlektüre und ist als solche in der gesamten angelsächsischen Welt bekannt.

Dieter Hamblock

Inhalt

Englische Romane

IN RECLAMS UNIVERSAL-BIBLIOTHEK

Jane Austen: Emma. 560 S. UB 7633 – Kloster Northanger. 296 S. UB 7728 – Mansfield Park. 572 S. UB 8007 – Stolz und Vorurteil. 460 S. UB 9871 – Überredung. 320 S. UB 7972 – Verstand und Gefühl. 431 S. UB 7836 – Alle sechs Romane auch in Kassette.

Charlotte Brontë: Jane Eyre. 816 S. UB 8647

Emily Brontë: Sturmhöhe. 470 S. UB 8279 – auch geb.

Lewis Carroll: Alices Abenteuer im Wunderland. 199 S. UB 9746 – Durch den Spiegel und was Alice dort fand. 211 S. UB 9747

Joseph Conrad: Herz der Finsternis. 167 S. UB 8714

Charles Dickens: Große Erwartungen 752 S. UB 562 – auch geb. – Schwere Zeiten. 430 S. UB 1308 – Der Weihnachtsabend. 120 S. UB 788

George Eliot: Middlemarch. 1176 S. UB 8080 – Die Mühle am Floss. 759 S. UB 2711

Oliver Goldsmith: Der Pfarrer von Wakefield. 237 S. UB 285

Thomas Hardy: Tess von den d'Urbervilles. 630 S. UB 9935

Nathaniel Hawthorne: Der scharlachrote Buchstabe. 336 S. UB 9454

Mary Shelley: Frankenstein oder Der moderne Prometheus. 327 S. UB 8357

Laurence Sterne: Tristram Shandy. 794 S. Geb.

Robert Louis Stevenson: Die Schatzinsel. 278 S. UB 4856

Jonathan Swift: Gullivers Reisen. 488 S. 16 Abb. UB 651 – auch geb.

Mark Twain: Die Abenteuer des Huckleberry Finn. 443 S. UB 3749

Oscar Wilde: Das Bildnis des Dorian Gray. 336 S. UB 5008 – auch geb.

Rudyard Kipling: *The Jungle Book.* 219 S. UB 9244

John le Carré: *Call for the Dead.* 240 S. UB 9048

Doris Lessing: *Three African Stories.* 77 S. UB 9245 – *To Room Nineteen.* 72 S. UB 9151

Katherine Mansfield: *The Garden-Party.* Five Short Stories. 85 S. UB 9152

W. Somerset Maugham: *The Letter.* 75 S. UB 9183 – *Rain.* 88 S. UB 9061

Ian McEwan: *The Cement Garden.* 182 S. UB 9069

A. A. Milne: *Winnie-the-Pooh.* Ill. 180 S. UB 9231

George Orwell: *England Your England and Other Essays.* 122 S. UB 9024

Rosamunde Pilcher: *Snow in April.* 262 S. UB 9017

Salman Rushdie: *East, West.* 275 S. UB 9094

Alan Sillitoe: *The Loneliness of the Long-distance Runner.* 88 S. UB 9192 – *Saturday Night and Sunday Morning.* 360 S. UB 9038

Muriel Spark: *The Prime of Miss Jean Brodie.* 189 S. UB 9193

Robert Louis Stevenson: *The Bottle Imp.* 59 S. UB 9157 – *The Strange Case of Dr. Jekyll and Mr. Hyde.* 119 S. UB 9167 – *Treasure Island.* Ill. 334 S. UB 9258

J. R. R. Tolkien: *Farmer Giles of Ham.* Ill. 112 S. UB 9025

Urban Legends. 104 S. UB 9065

Evelyn Waugh: *The Loved One.* 192 S. UB 9233

Fay Weldon: *The Fat Woman's Joke.* 216 S. UB 9028

H. G. Wells: *The Invisible Man.* 270 S. UB 9013 – *The Time Machine.* 160 S. UB 9176

Oscar Wilde: *The Canterville Ghost.* 64 S. UB 9177 – *The Happy Prince and Other Tales.* 91 S. UB 9293 – *The Picture of Dorian Gray.* 344 S. UB 9019

Virginia Woolf: *Mrs Dalloway's Party.* A Short Story Sequence. 93 S. UB 9196

Philipp Reclam jun. Stuttgart